100 Stoic Affirmations

1) Misfortunes are an inherent and inevitable part of life. Therefore, aware of this, Always remember that there are things that you can control and others that you cannot. Accept the things that cannot be change, and be kind to yourself about its.

2) Wise people are able to completely suspend their desire and turn their aversion solely toward what is under their full control. Knowing this will help me become more focused and able to accomplish anything.

3) Virtuous people accept and perform without any protest the role that Nature has assigned them. I affirm that I am Virtuous and worthy of the role that I am to play in shaping the world I live in.

4) Whatever happens to me is necessary for the fulfillment of my higher destiny. Knowing this allows me to strive to accomplish any goal without fear of failure, for the universe is with me.

5) Wisdom means aligning one's will with that of Universal Nature. By aligning my will I can focus my attention with fearless determination. Being positive that my goals will be attained.

6) Everything that happens is thought by Nature to benefit the whole of which I am a part. With this knowledge all my actions will be treated as part of the bigger picture. Knowing that I am not alone on my journey gives me strength and a sense of belonging.

7) Nature has equipped me with inner resources that can enable me to endure any adversity. Using these resources such as mediation and mindfulness will

help bring the meta and physical world to perfect alignment. Allowing me to function at the highest level.

8)   Truly virtuous people are revealed in difficult times. These difficult times also allow me as a person to grow, so when facing adversity, I will move forward and never backwards. Attacking life fiercely with the bravo of a Lion on a hunt.

9)   Wise people cheerfully embrace whatever The Universe sends their way. Knowing this allows me to see truly what adversity is, and how I may grow and hone my characteristics. Keeping a smile on my face no matter what adversity comes, because I know that it is what I need and not something that can break me.

10) Nature assigns the most difficult challenges to those for whom it has high hopes. With this knowledge I will keep my spirits high in the times of challenges. My high hopes will be contagious to those around me, allowing the entire group to become Enlighted in times of challenges, instead of allowing morale to crumble I will single handedly rebuild it if necessary. Because I am stronger than my circumstances.

11) Luck is like a pendulum that constantly swings back and forth. So, I know that I cannot have luck on my side daily sometimes it will be against me, this does not mean that I cannot stir up some internal fortitude and break through the bad luck that may seem to drift over head at times. Always

remember like any storm it will eventually pass.

12) Nothing prevents something bad that happened to another person from happening to me. Knowing this I will always be alert of my surroundings, never allowing my guard to be completely down. For a sunny day can become a battlefield in the blink of an eye. I am always ready for this battle no matter when.

13) Every habit is strengthened by repetition. So, I will only do things that benefit my well-being, leaving the vices that chain you behind. Repeating the things that strengthen me daily will make me stronger every day.

14) Most people perform vicious actions because they are confused about what is really "good" and "evil". To ensure that I walk on the side of "good" I need to merely listen to my heart and follow its guidance. Meditating on action if I am concerned of its true nature.

15) It is not possible to argue or fight alone. Knowing this if a situation arises where someone is trying to tempt me into anger or rage, I will merely disengage for I know the trap they are setting, I also know that there is a rage in that person that they most likely are not aware of. Like a child throwing a tantrum I will not fault them.

16) Forgiving someone who makes a mistake is a uniquely human trait. Knowing this means that to forgive someone for their transgressions is one of the highest forms of empathy. For to truly forgive we have to understand where the person is coming

from.

17) As a human being, I am not a wild beast but a rational creature. As a rational creature I will react only to the logical feelings that come up in me. I will not react to the internal animalistic actions such as revenge or physical violence, unless truly necessary.

18) We humans are all brothers and sisters. Therefore, aware of this, I promise to always be as tolerant and compassionate as possible toward others.

19) Anxiety is the natural result of giving too much importance to externals outside of one's control. Knowing that there are many things that I cannot control, I should focus my attention to the things that can be changed. Understanding that sometimes in life there will be struggle, but I can always overcome struggle. I will come out of it stronger than ever before.

20) The only effective cure for anxiety is the constant study and practice of philosophy. With the knowledge of the philosophers before me, I can overcome any challenge. The wisdom that the Stoics such as Seneca provides is wisdom that can never be underutilized. When I feel especially anxious I should think, "What would the Stoics do."

21) Anxiety stems from one's way of observing and interpreting reality. With this knowledge I should do my best to interpret reality through a positive glass, tend to forgive instead of place blame. Also observe that things are almost never what they appear at first. So take a mindful approach when observing things that seem hectic or chaotic at first.

22) Pursuing pleasure as if it were "good" and fleeing pain as if it were "evil" inevitably leads to living overwhelmed by anxiety. Therefore understanding that pain is as necessary as it is to breath, I will instead understand that pain is essential to my growth as a human being.

23) As a human being, I have full control over my mind and thoughts. This is one of the only things that I can truly control, although it may seem difficult at first, I know that I can view even the most daunting experiences as beneficial in some way and attempt to change my personal viewpoint. Being able to do so is a true glimpse into Enlightenment.

24) A mind that does not worry about the future and is totally focused on the present cannot experience anxiety. With this knowledge I will be mindful and present on any task in front of me. This will bring my mind from chaos to peacefulness, if there is nothing to be mindful about now, I can always bring myself back to my breath. Being mindful and just breathing will bring me into the moment.

25) We humans were designed by Nature to live in harmony with each other. Living as though your actions will affect another person can greatly improve my own life and the lives close to me. People will see that I genially care about their well-being and will

choose to do the same for me. Ensuring humanity is stronger in that moment.

26) Human beings are rational and social beings. Though it may at times not seem as such. If I react rationally to most chaotic events I will be the one who prospers through the chaos and into the light.

27) True revenge consists in responding to vice with vice. Therefore, aware of this, I promise to respond to any wrong with virtue. If I am virtuous in all of my actions I will never regret the actions of my past.

28) The human soul degrades itself when it says something false. By being truthful in all my discussions, I will ensure that my soul is not tainted with the filth of lies. And instead, be a shining example to those who see.

29) The human soul degrades itself when it betrays the trust of another person. To ensure that my soul is pure I shall never intentionally abuse the trust given to me by another person. This will help ensure a happy path without anyone seeking revenge or hate.

30) The human soul degrades itself when it turns its back on another person. Knowing this I will attempt to provide empathy to those who are in need, and to never turn a shoulder to someone in need if my cup is over filled.

31) The human soul degrades itself when it does injustice. To avoid degrading myself I will only respond to others in only a behavior that I believe is righteous, this will ensure that I stay pure and at peace with myself. For being righteous is one way to ensure that my life remains pure.

32) The human soul degrades itself when it intentionally harms another person. Harming another human being is essentially harming your own family members, as everyone who shares this earth is a part of your own family. With this view in mind, I can calm my anger towards any other person, with a calm mind I can see through any troubled storm. Ensuring I only portray a feeling of love to all other humans, avoiding any intentional harm to anyone.

33) Fame, money, power, etcetera, are empty things. I will not allow these things to influence my decisions and ethics as a person. These objects must be regarded carefully, as they may attempt to pull me into directions that are not pure. Remembering that these items are empty in themselves will help me detach the meaning from them and enable me to gain or lose these objects without becoming obsessed. Meditating on these subjects will also provide clarity.

34) Wise people are morally incorruptible. They cannot be bought at any price. I will also align myself with these morals, allowing corruption to enter my thoughts would corrupt my soul, I will always stick to my own morals and evaluate every situation through my own eyes and not the lens of corruption.

35) As a human being, nothing can prevent me from developing a character of integrity and virtue. I will always, attempt to align myself with virtue. Being virtuous in every situation will prevent myself from getting off track with Nature.

36) Wise people are those who value the health of their soul more than the health of their body. While I promise to maintain my body as well as possible, I will also treat the health of my mind and soul as equally important, a great body with a soured mind is no benefit to anyone. Having a pure mind and pure body is as close to heaven as possible.

37) The more one values things outside of one's control, the less control one has. I will only focus my mind on the situations that I know I can control, to focus on things out of my control will cause anxiety and useless worrying. I can change my view on my thoughts and not much else. So, focus within if in chaos.

38) As a human being, I do not have control over external events. The only thing I can control are my responses to them. Knowing this I will ensure that my reposes are those that inspire peace and hopefulness. If someone offers me a closed fist, I will offer only peace and love. Until absolutely necessary I will be as a cloud floating through the sky, if the situation calls for it though I will unleash a tornado from that same peaceful cloud.

39) Unwise people are weak and always seek help from others. Wise people are strong and seek help from themselves. Therefore, when in chaos I will seek for the answers inside myself, for the solution is always there. If I need to seek help from others, I will ensure those others have my best interest in mind.

40) Unwise people are weak and always blame others. Wise people are strong and look for blame in themselves. In any situation that I seek to blame someone first look internally to ensure that I can improve everything that is possible for myself.

41) As a human being, the only thing Nature has made me responsible for is the proper use of the mind and its faculties.

Knowing this I will use my mind and facilities to better human race at any available opportune. Leaving the world better than when I found it is one of the most noble paths a person can follow.

42) The gods have made me strong enough to bravely endure all that is beyond my control and responsible only for that under my full control. Therefore, I will always head into chaos with my head up and know that I can conquer any hard time that is ahead of me. I also know that these trials will only make me a better person.

43) I cannot escape death. The only thing I can do is eradicate my fear of it. Fearing death is only a constraint that is useless to allow to affect me, for it is one of the unavoidable processes of life. Living life to the fullest is one of the best ways to conquer any fears of death.

44) Death is nothing more than the event that marks the separation of body and soul. Being aware of this allows me to not free the event its self and live life in a way that is fulfilling to me.

45) My time on this Earth is limited. I do not have infinite years ahead of me. Death could come at any moment. When I look into the void of death all I can do is smile back, for the time that has been made available to me, may not be awarded to someone else.

46) Wise people find joy in living but at the same time are not reluctant to die. In order to find joy in life mindfulness will assist me on being present every moment I possibly can which will enhance the experience I have on earth.

47) Death is a natural process necessary for the Universe to continue to evolve. Knowing this I can find peace when a close one reaches the end of their road, because I know that this process is completely natural and a necessary part for life to begin. I find solace in the fact that life must always have a beginning and an end.

48) Life is like a play: what matters is not its length, but its quality. A life well lived can have quality to it that a short story may have, there are many masterpieces that are only a couple of pages long, live life like that curtains may drop at any moment and the quality of my life will be one of a great masterpiece no matter the length.

49) As a human being, I am born to remain indifferent to external events and act with virtue. With this knowledge I will be virtuous even when my enemy is not, with this virtue I will be victorious in any battle no matter what the outcome.

50) We humans were created to work and create, not to laze around and indulge in pleasure. Therefore, if there is no work that is apparent, I will make work and strive to create new ideas. I can use this as an outlet to express myself in many different ways.

51) Virtuous people stick to the mission that Nature has assigned them as if it were an inviolable law. I will always move in the direction that I feel that mission is pulling me towards. As long as my path is virtuous and noble I can never go astray.

52) As a human being, I have the duty to follow the natural laws written by the Universe. The laws are the same ones that every being must abide by. I will intentionally look towards the stars when I need to be reminded that the Universe has a plan.

53) As a rational and conscious creature, I have the duty of assisting Universal Nature in the realization of its divine evolutionary plan. With this knowledge I will always seek to expand my knowledge and assist fellow beings on their journey at any opportunity.

54) There is nothing more important than accepting what Fate sends and obeying the orders imparted by one's spirit. Therefore, whenever anything comes my way, even if it seems treacherous at first I know that it is only going to improve my character, for what could be more righteous than destiny.

55) For those who follow Nature, life is simple and full of joy. For those who resist Nature, life is complicated and full of pain. Knowing this I will seek to align myself with the Natural rhythm of life, going with the flow of energy instead of trying to fight against it. At times being like a stone on a river bed slowly moving down stream, even as a roaring river flows overhead, I gently roll down stream.

56) Whoever undertakes a project without the Universe's approval is doomed to fail and suffer. But if the project is one that is for the Universe's betterment than it will succeed, even if it may not seem like it at first. I know that the Will of the Universe is with me.

57) Virtuous people perform willingly and cheerfully whatever mission Universal Nature assigns them. No matter what job I am currently doing, I know that it is what I am supposed to be doing. Therefore I can do my tasks with mindfulness and be happy in the duties that I perform.

58) Every single event is the right one to fulfill both my personal destiny and that of the Universe as a whole. I will approach every event with a positive attitude and complete tasks with the utmost sincerity. Always maintaining a positive mental attitude.

59) Noble spirits are recognizable by their unconditional acceptance of reality, degenerate spirits by their unconditional rejection of reality. Reality and the views that I take on situations will greatly affect my mental state, I will always accept what is truth, and never shy away from it even if at first it is difficult.

60) As a rational and conscious creature, I have the duty of trying to interpret the divine design of The Universe in order to align my actions with it. Therefore, aware of this, I promise to do my best to fulfill this duty of mine.

61) Freedom is not achieved by satisfying desire but by eliminating it. In minimizing the things that I "want", by realizing that most "wants" are only material objects and will only chain me to them. This will allow me to be free from vices that would normally keep me down.

62) No one can force me to think, say, or do something that my own spirit does not approve. I will never allow someone to force me to take any action that I do not deem virtuous, I will see through their veils and see their actions for what it is. I will distance myself from those who would attempt to taint my soul with lies and deceit.

63) Wise people know that true freedom consists in doing what Nature commands and in accepting what the Universe sends. With this knowledge I know that I am born with freedom and slowly choose to give it away through time. I will always seek to follow the destiny in front of me and never try to veer away from the path that I know is best.

64) As a human being, I am part of Nature, and nothing can stop me from acting in harmony with it. I will always seek to be harmonious with the Universe and Nature, because it is the only way to be interconnected with everything.

65) Bodily impulses are the main obstacle to the virtuous exercise of free will. Therefore, I will think clearly about my actions and ensure that I do not act on impulses for many mistakes are made when one acts without thought or concern. If I feel that my state of mind is not one that is ready to act, I will meditate on the subject before acting.

66) As a human being, Universal Nature has given me the greatest gift of all: free will. Therefore, aware of this, I promise to use it wisely. Free Will is something that can be used for great good or evil, I will always aim to do what is righteous and virtuous.

67) Those who are properly grounded in life do not feel the need to seek approval outside of themselves. Seeking others approval will only lead to a path of constant anxiety, people opinions change very often,

I do not have to concern myself with their opinions, because tomorrow it will be a different one anyways.

68) If something is right, it remains so regardless of popular opinion. I will always do what I feel is right regardless of the people around me opinions. The truth is the truth no matter who says it and what's right is right no matter who does it.

69) Wise people are indifferent to both compliments and insults. Therefore, I will take what people say regarding this with a grain of salt. For I know that people who compliment are usually doing so for gain, and those who insult are usually doing it out of spite. Either way I will remain steadfast in my own work.

70) In most cases, following the crowd leads to ignorant and vicious actions. Therefore, aware of this, I promise to always make my decisions freely and independently.

71) The unwise crowd tends to assign the highest value to things like wealth, power, social status, and so on. Seeing this fact for what it is, I will stride to place my highest value on morals and knowledge as the highest values, for material objects only cause constraints.

72) True philosophers do not feel obliged to respect the popular opinion about what is "good & evil" and "right & wrong". Knowing this I will analyze what I view as "good & evil" and I will act on what I deem good. If the decision is one that seems difficult I will meditate on the subject until I arrive at an answer.

73) Happiness comes from within and is completely independent of external circumstances. Knowing this empowers me to be with happiness and peace no matter what situation I may be in currently. I know that I can change my views of the situation, even if I cannot change the current situation physically. Where my thoughts flow my energy goes.

74) By virtue of human nature, it is not possible to achieve happiness by leading a selfish and vicious life. I will promise to be selfless in this life and tend to my fellow people with empathy and compassion, for we are all on a difficult journey at times.

75) True happiness comes from living a harmonious life. Power and wealth have nothing to do with it. Although at times I may possess power and wealth if the Universe commands it, I know that these things may also be taken back if the Universe commands it. Therefore, I will always be true to myself and harmonious with others. This will ensure happiness during any tide of life.

76) True happiness is a by-product of wisdom. Therefore, I will seek the wisdom of the ancients before me. Also, I will seek my own wisdom from living life and learning day by day. For the greatest knowledge to obtain is from seeing it with my own eyes. Reading is always fine, but for me to really learn the lesson I must apply it in life and with action.

77) A mind whose thoughts are obsessively directed toward the past or the future cannot be happy. I will be mindful and present in every moment. Worrying about the past or things to come will only cause more worry than is necessary. I will leave the past in the past and greet the future with open arms no matter what I may

perceive. For it will be what the Universe commands either way.

78) Giving importance to other people's judgment is one of the main sources of unhappiness. Therefore, aware of this, I promise to train my mind so that it becomes independent and seeks approval only from itself. I will instead look inside myself for what I deem as right and virtuous.

79) Rage is weakness. True strength consists in calmness and serenity. Therefore, I will be the calm in the storm, I will not react to anger. I know that any action I do out of anger will lead to regret. I will be strong and react only when necessary and always with the appropriate response for each occasion.

80) By its very nature, the human mind is capable of enduring anything. I know that no matter how difficult the situation may seem at the moment, I can handle any obstacle. I know that I will always succeed and persevere for I am unstoppable.

81) True strength is a peace of mind that cannot be disturbed by anything or anyone. I will keep my mind calm and peaceful as a gentle summer breeze or a small cloud floating on a sunny day. This calmness will come from my virtuous way of life, I know that Nature is on the side of the harmonious and I am harmonious with the Universe.

82) Unwise people try to conquer the outside world. Wise people try to conquer themselves. Conquering my mind will allow me to bring myself back to peace whenever I am stirred. I will look to the inside instead of those on the outside whenever I seek guidance. For the answer is usually already known inside me.

83) Nothing that happens can hurt me unless I interpret it happening as harmful to me. I will perceive challenges as beneficial for what else could show me who I truly am, but challenging times. The way that I react during chaos will show that I am truly virtuous and righteous. Anyone can be righteous during peace, but those who can provide light in the darkness are truly at peace.

84) The human mind knows no needs except those it creates for itself. Therefore, I will strive to keep my mind pure in thought and only focus on the thoughts that are positive and helpful. Letting those thoughts that are not positive float away like clouds in the sky, seeing them for what they are and letting them go.

85) The Universe in which we live is made up of opposites in harmony with each other. Therefore, just because something may seem like it is vastly different, does not mean that I cannot be in harmony with it and live with peace. I must be accepting of all walks of life for it is not my job to pass judgment.

86) The world is what it is. No amount of complaining will ever change its nature. Only action can change anything, therefore, I will not complain about the way things are. Instead, I will attempt to change what I see is wrong. People will see the actions I perform as righteous and virtuous, this will inspire them to change as well.

87) The Logos that governs the universe knows no evil

and always has the good of the whole at heart. Knowing this I will also attempt to keep my actions harmonious with others. I will seek to spread hope and peace to all other creatures I meet. Knowing that we are all connected in many different ways.

88) The world is nothing but change. All is transitory. Nothing is forever. Knowing this I shall remain adaptable to whatever situation arises, I will also not fear change for I know that it is the true nature of the Universe. Without constant change there can be no new life, I am aware of this and I welcome change.

89) Behind the entire Universe lies one soul and one purpose. Everything that exists is interconnected. Knowing this I know that if I seek harm to another, I also seek harm to myself. I will instead seek to empower others and improve their well-being, for doing so will also empower me.

90) As a human being, I am a child of Nature. Knowing this I shall always seek to be harmonious with the will of Nature. I will also provide assistance to Nature whenever I can, Because I know that this Nature that I come from must survive and thrive for new life to begin.

91) Mental suffering is the result of an incorrect interpretation of reality. Knowing this I will always look inside myself when I feel that I am suffering. I know that sometimes I must change the views and opinions that I come up with to bring myself back to peace. I will ensure that I am viewing situations in a positive light.

92) Trying to run away from pain is a vicious act, for it means not living in harmony with the nature of things. I know that sometimes pain is necessary for growth, I will not turn and run when things get tough. Instead I will run towards the pain and embrace it for what it is, which is a stepping stone in my path to greatness.

93) Divine nature is completely indifferent to pain. Therefore, I will also be indifferent towards pain. I know that change can sometimes bring pain, I will not allow it to affect the way that I am feeling, nor will I allow it to make me respond with anger. Instead, I will be calm even when in pain, this show true strength.

94) Nothing is painful when taken lightly. Therefore, if it is a conversation that has caused me pain, I will take their opinion lightly and allow the comments to fall away from me like leave from a tree.

95) Pain is an intrinsic part of life. Therefore, aware of this, I recognize that there is no point in fearing something from which there is no escape. Instead, I will approach it fearlessly and make my decisions based what I see fit for the situation. I will not let pain or fear determine my actions.

96) Divine nature is completely indifferent to pleasure. Therefore, I will not seek to fill my life completely with pleasure, too much pleasure will lead to addiction. Do not overindulge in the things that bring me pleasure, for this will only lead to losing the pleasure.

97) Trying to pursue pleasure is a vicious act, for it means not living in harmony with human nature. I will allow pleasure to come to me, but to pursue it constantly will only instead lead to pain. I will be

mindful in the things that bring me immense pleasure, I realize that they may be taken at any moment and will cherish them while here, but will not mourn if they are taken away.

98) The human mind has the ability to tame any impulse generated by the body. Knowing this I will not allow impulses to be the only factor of my decisions. I know that the mind has great power over impulses and the rational mind will prevail if I train it to do so.

99) Anything taken to the excess becomes a vice. Therefore, aware of this, I promise to indulge in material pleasures just enough to keep my body strong and healthy, not to the point where I become enamored and chained to these pleasures.

100) In the long run, resisting the temptation of a pleasure brings far more satisfaction than indulging in it. Therefore, aware of this, I promise to always think twice before impulsively giving in to pleasure.

101) Spiritual progress does not happen overnight. With this knowledge I will strive to improve myself mentally and spiritually daily. After making progress day after day, I know that I will eventually see the results of my discipline. This gives me the strength to carry through adverse times.

102) The first step toward spiritual progress is to get rid of all the false beliefs that confuse one's mind. I will not blindly

follow the advice given to me, instead I will always look inward on advice given, to ensure that what is being given is true advice. Some people will give bad advice on purpose, knowing this I will always examine my beliefs.

103) As a human being, nothing can stop me from changing those character traits that lead me to say or do vicious things. Knowing this I must be the example for others to follow. I will always stick to my values and morals, no matter what the common crowd is doing. The wise man usually walks alone and not with the crowd.

104) Wise people in order to avoid vice constantly keep an eye on themselves as if they were their own enemy lying in ambush. Knowing this I must be constantly vigilant with my own thoughts. Even these thoughts can begin to cause anxiety if the mind is allowed to stray. I will be mindful when in chaos, bringing my mind to peace the rest will follow.

105) Surrounding myself with virtuous people leads to becoming virtuous,

intermingling with vicious people leads to becoming vicious. Knowing this I will choose my friends wisely. The wrong people can possibly lead to unneeded temptations, I will evaluate my relationships and ensure that the people I spend my time with have my best interest in mind.

106) Studying philosophy books is not enough. Virtue can only be cultivated through unremitting practice. I will take action in the real world with all the lessons I learn from ancients, the world needs action and not more books to read, I will strive to achieve greatness for men and women to inspire too.

107) When I encounter unkindness, I understand that the person who is presenting this unkindness is most likely in a painful position in their life. Hurt people tend to hurt people, knowing this I will respond to anger with empathy and compassion. This act will have a positive effect me as well as the other person.

108) Everything depends on how I view it, if I view challenges as beneficial than I will instead look forward to obstacles. Looking forward to these challenges will give me strength instead of anxiety about change, for without challenges or change how can I possibly improve.

109) My mind should sit superior to my body and its sensations
I will not allow pain, loss of appetite, or any other sensations, if I feel that I am almost giving in to it I will meditate and bring my mind back to peace. The worldly sensations cannot affect me if my mind is strong.

110) I will be mindful and deliberate in all actions that I take. Instead of allowing my focus to be drawn to things that have no purpose, I will keep my mind focused with the discipline of a warrior on the battlefield.

111) I will not retreat from the world, no

matter how my view of people may be altered from time to time. I will instead march into the world fearless, for I understand that bad things may happen, but I am willing to face anything the world has to offer, for what else could be my destiny.

112) I will avoid complaining, this will solve nothing. If I have a problem instead of restating the problem, I will look for a solution to the problem. If I can find the answer to the problem then there is no reason to complain in the first place.

113) I will confine myself to the present moment, for this is nothing else. I will not allow my mind to wonder to the future or the past, for they are the roots of anxiety and depression.

114) When I arise in the morning, I will think about how great a privilege it is to be alive, to breathe, to think and to enjoy. I will then take this positivity and let in blend into the rest of my actions. Each day that I am blessed with is another opportunity to do great things.

115) No man is free who is not a master of himself. With this knowledge I will look to better myself and control the emotions inside me. I will respond to my emotions with a calculated response.

116) Men are disturbed not by the situations, but the view on which they take on these situations. I will do my best to ensure that my outlook is positive, because I know that I can accomplish any task I choose to.

117) It is the nature of the wise to resist pleasures, but the foolish to be a slave to them. With this knowledge I will only strive for the items that I truly need, I will not expend energy on useless items that will not be of any use in the future. Items of the world tend to require more time than they are worth in the end.

118) How ridiculous and how strange to be surprised at anything which happens in life. Knowing this I will expect the unexpected I will be vigilant and not

react with panic when situations go unexpected. I will instead respond with a calm and steady attitude. Chaos is a side effect of change, so always expect that it may appear at any moment.

119) To be calm is the highest achievement of the self. With this knowledge I will seek to be the calm in the storm. I am the master of my emotions and can choose to be calm in instances where others would lose their calm.

120) Choose not to be harmed by comments and you won't feel harmed. Don't feel harm and you haven't been. No matter what the situation I know that I have the power to change my perspective towards situations If I view them as what they are then they will have no effect on me. That is what I will choose when uneasy situations occur.

121) Be tolerant with others and strict with yourself, for the choices that you

make will influence your life. I know that every decision I make will have a compounding effect. If I make small and positive changes over time, they will equate to massive changes later in life.

122) Don't explain your philosophy, embody it. I will always strive to show the right way more than trying to explain what is right. If people, see that I am doing all the right things than they too will strive for greatness. This will have a positive effect on the world.